Study Guide for Decoding The Scarlet Letter

With Typical Questions and Answers

Steven Smith

Sherwood Press

Contents

1

HOW TO USE THIS GUIDE

This analysis of The Scarlet Letter intends to offer a study guide to readers who need a more in-depth view of the story.

This book is divided into questions, so the answers appear in a short essay style and may include repeated information. The questions are typical of what a high school student may experience.

I want to think all important questions have been either directly or indirectly answered. However, if you, the reader, feel something is missing, please reach out to me, and I will add it!

Happy studying!

Steven Smith
stevensmithvo@gmail.com
www.classicbooksexplained.com

Historical background of Nathanial Hawthorne and his novel The Scarlet Letter

Nathaniel Hawthorne was born on July 4, 1804, in Salem, Massachusetts. His ancestors were some of the earliest settlers of the New England colonies, and his great-great-grandfather, John Hathorne, was one of the judges at the infamous Salem Witch Trials of 1692.

This connection to one of the darkest moments in American Puritanical history influenced Hawthorne greatly, making him aware of the intolerance and strict religious orthodoxy of his ancestors. He added a "w" to his last name, distancing himself from his ancestors' shameful past, and dedicated much of his literary work to examining the complexities and moral ambiguities of the human spirit, especially as it was manifested in Puritan New England.

Hawthorne was a contemporary of other prominent American authors such as Edgar Allan Poe and Herman Melville. He attended Bowdoin College in Maine, where he became friends with future President Franklin Pierce. After college, he spent twelve years writing and living at home with his mother, a period he referred to as his "dark years".

"The Scarlet Letter" was published in 1850 and is set in 17th-century Puritan Boston. It tells the story of Hester Prynne, a woman who conceives a child through an affair and struggles to create a new life of dignity and repentance in a strict Puritan society. Hester is forced to wear a scarlet "A" on her dress as a symbol of her sin: adultery. The novel delves deeply into the human experiences of guilt, sin, and legalism.

The book draws on the history and social norms of Puritan New England that Hawthorne was familiar with due to his own heritage. He also utilized his understanding of the human condition and the moral struggles that individuals face. For instance, Reverend Dimmesdale, who is revealed to be the father of Hester's child, grapples with his own guilt and hypocrisy. This intense psychological focus on characters was one of Hawthorne's signature writing traits and contributed significantly to the Dark Romanticism literary movement.

"The Scarlet Letter" was a critical success and helped to establish Hawthorne as a significant literary figure. The book remains an important part of the American literary canon and is frequently studied in high school and university literature courses for its exploration of themes such as guilt, sin, the nature of evil, and the conflict between societal expectations and personal beliefs. Despite this, Hawthorne himself was not particularly happy with the novel's popularity, stating in a letter to a friend, "I do not think much of them," referring to his novels, and wished he could write "better books."

Nathaniel Hawthorne died in his sleep on May 19, 1864. Despite his humble self-assessment, his works, particularly "The Scarlet Letter," have had a lasting impact on American literature, helping to shape its themes and narrative style.

What are the historical references in the novel

"The Scarlet Letter" is a work of historical fiction that uses numerous historical references to create a realistic portrayal of Puritan society in 17th-century New England. Here are some examples:

1. **The Setting**: The novel is set in mid-17th century Boston, then a Puritan settlement. The customs, dress, architecture, and laws of the town reflect the realities of Puritan New England during this time.

2. **Puritan Beliefs and Practices**: The novel frequently references the religious beliefs and practices of the Puritans, who were a religious group that believed in strict moral and religious codes. The public shaming of Hester Prynne, for instance, is a reflection of how Puritan society dealt with those who broke its laws (Hawthorne, 1850, Ch. 2).

3. **Historical Figures**: The novel references several real historical figures. For example, Governor Bellingham, who is a character in the novel, was a real person and a colonial governor of Massachusetts. The same goes for Mistress Hibbins, who is portrayed as a witch in the novel; she was a real person who was executed for witchcraft in Salem (Hawthorne, 1850, Ch. 8).

4. **Anne Hutchinson**: Hawthorne references Anne Hutchinson,

a religious dissenter in the Massachusetts Bay Colony who was banished for her beliefs. Hester's questioning of Puritan norms and her subsequent punishment echo Hutchinson's experiences (Hawthorne, 1850, Ch. 1).

5. **King's Chapel**: The novel refers to King's Chapel, a real historical site in Boston, where the Reverend Mr. Wilson preaches (Hawthorne, 1850, Ch. 3).

6. **The Witch Trials**: The fear of witchcraft, a prevalent concern in Puritan New England, is referenced in the character of Mistress Hibbins, who is said to be a witch. This reflects the historical reality of the Salem Witch Trials, which occurred in the late 17th century (Hawthorne, 1850, Ch. 8).

These historical references lend authenticity to the novel and situate its story within a specific time and place, grounding its exploration of universal themes like sin, guilt, and redemption in a concrete historical context.

Why do students read The Scarlet Leter

"The Scarlet Letter" by Nathaniel Hawthorne is often included in high school and university curricula for several reasons:

1. **Historical Context**: The novel offers a window into the Puritan era of American history, a period that had a profound impact on American culture and societal norms. Students can learn about the beliefs, societal structure, and moral code of the time, which were integral to the formation of the American identity.

2. **Exploration of Themes**: "The Scarlet Letter" deals with complex themes such as sin, guilt, redemption, identity, societal norms, hypocrisy, and individual versus collective morality. These themes are universal and timeless, allowing students to engage with the text on multiple levels and apply its lessons to their own lives.

3. **Character Development**: The characters in "The Scarlet Letter" are deeply complex and undergo significant development throughout the novel. For instance, Hester Prynne, initially shamed and ostracized, evolves into a resilient, independent, and ultimately respected woman in her community. Reverend Dimmesdale's character arc exposes the debilitating effects of hidden guilt and hypocrisy. This exploration of character provides an opportunity for students to study character development and motivations.

4. **Literary Techniques**: Hawthorne's novel is rich in literary techniques and devices, including symbolism, foreshadowing, and irony. The scarlet letter "A" itself is a powerful symbol of sin, shame, and, eventually, strength and defiance. The novel is also an excellent example of the Romantic, and more specifically, Dark Romantic genre, featuring the examination of human nature's darker side.

5. **Critical Thinking**: Reading and analyzing "The Scarlet Letter" requires and develops critical thinking skills. Students are prompted to question the societal norms of the Puritan era, the actions and motivations of the characters, and the implications of the novel's themes in the present context.

6. **Moral and Ethical Discussions**: The novel raises many ethical and moral questions. What is the nature of sin? How does society punish those who step out of bounds, and is this punishment effective or just? What is the effect of guilt on the human psyche? Such discussions can lead to a deeper understanding of ethics and morality in a societal and personal context.

In addition to these, the novel's position as a classic of American literature makes it a reference point in many literary discussions and a must-read for anyone studying American literature. Despite being written in the 19th century, "The Scarlet Letter" continues to offer relevant insights into societal norms, individual freedom, and the human condition, making it valuable for students today.

What are the historical contexts

The historical context of a novel refers to the social, political, and cultural conditions and events that surround the period when the book was written and set. Understanding this can help readers appreciate the circumstances and influences that impacted the author's narrative.

"The Scarlet Letter" by Nathaniel Hawthorne was published in 1850, but the story is set in the mid-17th century, specifically around the years 1642-1649, in a Puritan settlement in Boston.

Puritan Society: Puritans were a group of English Reformed Protestants who sought to "purify" the Church of England from what they considered to be residual Catholic practices. They were known for their strict moral and religious code. Adultery, the central sin in "The Scarlet Letter," was considered a grave offense, punishable by public shaming, which is reflected in the way Hester Prynne is treated.

The American Colonies: During the mid-17th century, Massachusetts was a British colony. Colonists often lived in tight-knit communities and followed strict laws, many of which were tied to religious practices. The novel portrays this aspect of colonial life, showing the significant influence of the community and religious leaders on individuals' lives.

The Role of Women: Women's roles in Puritan society were very restricted and centered around the home and the church. Women were expected to behave modestly and comply with religious laws. Any woman who transgressed these norms, like Hester Prynne, faced severe consequences.

Salem Witch Trials: Hawthorne's great-great-grandfather was a judge during the infamous Salem Witch Trials, a series of hearings and prosecutions of people accused of witchcraft in colonial Massachusetts between February 1692 and May 1693. Hawthorne's direct connection to these events, which were another example of the extremity of Puritanical society's norms and punishment, was a significant influence on his writings.

When Hawthorne wrote "The Scarlet Letter" in the mid-19th century, the United States was grappling with significant societal changes, including westward expansion, debates over slavery that would eventually lead to the Civil War, and a shifting cultural and moral landscape. All these elements likely informed the themes of sin, guilt, punishment, and redemption in "The Scarlet Letter".

References:

- Bremer, Francis J. (2009). "Puritanism: A Very Short Introduction". Oxford University Press.

- Hawthorne, Nathaniel. (1850). "The Scarlet Letter".

- Norton, Mary Beth. (2003). "In the Devil's Snare: The Salem Witchcraft Crisis of 1692". Vintage Books.

- Baker, Carlos. (1981). "Emerson Among the Eccentrics: A Group Portrait". Viking Adult.

Describe the character developments

"The Scarlet Letter" by Nathaniel Hawthorne provides a rich study of character development, with many of the primary characters undergoing significant changes throughout the course of the narrative. Here's a look at how the main characters develop:

1. Hester Prynne: At the start of the novel, Hester is presented as a woman guilty of adultery, condemned to wear the scarlet letter "A" on her chest as a constant reminder of her sin. Despite the public shaming and isolation, Hester remains strong and refuses to name her co-sinner. As the story progresses, Hester, who is initially a symbol of sin, transforms into a symbol of strength and resilience. She becomes a talented seamstress, provides for herself and her daughter Pearl, and helps the poor and sick, gradually gaining the respect of the community. By the end of the novel, Hester's scarlet letter, initially a sign of shame, has become a symbol of individuality and defiance against societal norms (Hawthorne, 1850, Ch. 13).

2. Arthur Dimmesdale: Dimmesdale is the town minister and the man with whom Hester had her affair. Unlike Hester, he keeps his sin hidden and suffers from debilitating guilt and shame throughout the novel. He tries to confess his sin on several occasions but lacks the courage. His guilt ultimately manifests as a physical ailment, symbolically represented by his clutching his heart in several scenes (Hawthorne, 1850, Ch. 11). His character arc ends with his public confession on the scaffold, where he reveals his own scarlet letter engraved on his chest, symbolizing his internalization of guilt (Hawthorne, 1850, Ch. 23).

3. **Roger Chillingworth**: Chillingworth, Hester's estranged husband, initially appears as a sympathetic character. However, his obsession with uncovering the identity of Hester's lover and seeking revenge leads him down a path of transformation into a sinister and malevolent figure. He manages to discover Dimmesdale's secret and torments him, further damaging Dimmesdale's physical and mental health. Chillingworth's transformation into a symbol of evil is complete by the end of the novel (Hawthorne, 1850, Ch. 14).

4. **Pearl**: Pearl, the illegitimate daughter of Hester and Dimmesdale, is a symbol of her mother's sin. Described as a mischievous and almost otherworldly child, Pearl constantly reminds her parents of their sin, particularly when she obsesses over the scarlet letter (Hawthorne, 1850, Ch. 15). As the novel progresses, Pearl grows more insightful, often articulating truths that the adults around her cannot. After Dimmesdale's confession and death, Pearl becomes more human and less a symbol of her parents' sin, demonstrating her development.

These character developments are essential to the narrative of "The Scarlet Letter", enhancing the plot and enriching the novel's exploration of guilt, punishment, and redemption.

Describe the literary techniques

Nathaniel Hawthorne employed various literary techniques in "The Scarlet Letter" to create depth and meaning in his narrative. Here are some notable examples:

1. Symbolism: Symbolism is a crucial device used throughout the novel, with objects, characters, and events holding a deeper meaning.

- The most prominent symbol is the scarlet letter "A" itself. Initially, it symbolizes 'Adultery' and serves as a token of public shame for Hester. As the novel progresses, it evolves to represent 'Able' or 'Angel,' symbolizing Hester's strength, resilience, and transformation (Hawthorne, 1850, Ch. 13).

- Pearl, Hester's daughter, is another significant symbol. She is a living embodiment of Hester's sin, a constant reminder of her transgression. However, she also symbolizes innocence and the potential for redemption (Hawthorne, 1850, Ch. 6).

- The scaffold is a symbol of public confession and punishment, a place where sin is acknowledged and condemned (Hawthorne, 1850, Ch. 12).

2. Irony: Hawthorne uses irony to underscore the hypocrisy and hidden evil in the Puritan society.

- For example, Dimmesdale, a revered minister, is the hidden sinner. His public image starkly contrasts with his private guilt

(Hawthorne, 1850, Ch. 11).

- Chillingworth, a doctor supposed to heal, instead inflicts emotional and psychological pain on Dimmesdale in revenge (Hawthorne, 1850, Ch. 14).

3. Foreshadowing: Hawthorne often hints at future events or reveals.

- Dimmesdale's frequent hand over his heart foreshadows his final revelation of the self-inflicted scarlet letter on his chest (Hawthorne, 1850, Ch. 23).

- The meteor forming an 'A' in the sky foreshadows Dimmesdale's connection to the scarlet letter (Hawthorne, 1850, Ch. 12).

4. Allegory: The novel is an allegory for the struggle between sin and redemption.

- Hester's public punishment contrasts with Dimmesdale's private guilt, symbolizing the struggle between public shame and internal guilt.

- The transformation of the meaning of the scarlet letter "A" represents the power of personal growth and redemption.

5. Imagery: Hawthorne uses vivid descriptive language to create mental pictures that assist in understanding the story.

- The description of the "ugly weeds" and the rosebush outside the prison in the first chapter sets the mood for the novel (Hawthorne, 1850, Ch. 1).

Describe how critical thinking is acheived by reading this novel

"The Scarlet Letter" by Nathaniel Hawthorne is an excellent novel to foster critical thinking due to its intricate narrative, complex characters, and exploration of themes. Here's how the novel contributes to developing critical thinking:

1. **Interpretation of Symbols**: Hawthorne's novel is filled with symbols, such as the scarlet letter "A", Pearl, the scaffold, and the meteor. These symbols often have multiple interpretations and evolve throughout the novel, requiring readers to constantly reassess their meanings. This process of interpretation encourages critical thinking.

2. **Understanding Characters**: The characters in "The Scarlet Letter" are complex and morally ambiguous. Analyzing their actions, motivations, and development requires careful thought and encourages readers to consider multiple perspectives.

3. **Examination of Themes**: The novel explores profound themes such as sin, guilt, identity, societal norms, and individual versus collective morality. Engaging with these themes requires readers to question their own beliefs and assumptions, fostering a deeper level of critical thinking.

4. **Evaluation of Societal Norms**: The Puritan society depicted in the novel was marked by strict rules and public shaming. By examining these practices, readers are prompted to critically analyze societal norms, both in the context of the novel and in their own societies.

5. Analysis of Historical Context: "The Scarlet Letter" is set in a specific historical period, requiring readers to understand the social, cultural, and political conditions of that era. Analyzing how these conditions influence the story and characters helps develop critical thinking.

6. Encouragement of Empathy: The characters' dilemmas and moral choices compel readers to put themselves in the characters' places, promoting empathy and the ability to understand different viewpoints.

7. Engagement with Moral and Ethical Questions: The novel raises important ethical and moral questions, such as the nature of sin, the role of punishment, the burden of guilt, and the possibility of redemption. Wrestling with these questions promotes a deeper level of thinking and self-reflection.

In these ways, "The Scarlet Letter" goes beyond being a historical novel, offering a fertile ground for readers to develop and practice critical thinking skills. By prompting readers to question, analyze, and reflect on the narrative, characters, and themes, the novel fosters an environment conducive to critical thought.

Describe the moral and ethical discussions of the novel

"The Scarlet Letter" by Nathaniel Hawthorne delves into various moral and ethical discussions. Here are some significant ones:

1. **Sin and Redemption**: The novel centers around the concept of sin, represented by Hester Prynne's act of adultery. However, Hawthorne suggests that acknowledging and living with one's sin, as Hester does, may lead to redemption, growth, and ultimately, a form of virtue (Hawthorne, 1850, Ch. 13). In contrast, Dimmesdale, who hides his sin, is tormented by guilt, indicating that unacknowledged or unconfessed sin can lead to self-destruction (Hawthorne, 1850, Ch. 20).

2. **Hypocrisy vs. Sincerity**: Hawthorne exposes the hypocrisy of Puritan society, where image and social standing often overshadow genuine virtue. Dimmesdale is a respected minister, yet he conceals his sin of adultery, highlighting the gap between public image and private morality (Hawthorne, 1850, Ch. 11). On the other hand, Hester, who openly wears the symbol of her sin, lives a life of sincerity and helpfulness, raising questions about what constitutes true virtue.

3. **Punishment and Justice**: Hester's public shaming and the permanent mark of the scarlet letter bring up the question of whether such a punishment is just for a personal and arguably victimless crime. This punishment contrasts sharply with the hidden guilt and torment of Dimmesdale, which he himself experiences as a form of internal punishment (Hawthorne, 1850, Ch. 12).

4. Individual Morality vs. Collective Morality: The novel examines the conflict between personal conscience and societal norms. Hester's act of adultery defies societal norms, yet she believes her love for Dimmesdale was genuine, raising the question of whether society or the individual gets to define morality (Hawthorne, 1850, Ch. 18).

5. The Role of Compassion: Hester, despite being ostracized, shows compassion throughout the novel. She helps the poor and sick and is there for Dimmesdale in his time of need, indicating that compassion and understanding can exist even in those whom society deems sinful (Hawthorne, 1850, Ch. 13).

6. Revenge and Forgiveness: Chillingworth's transformation into a figure of evil in his quest for revenge raises ethical questions about the destructive effects of revenge and the power of forgiveness. His actions lead to Dimmesdale's destruction and his own loss of humanity (Hawthorne, 1850, Ch. 14).

What is the tone of the novel

"The Scarlet Letter" is marked by a predominantly dark and serious tone, reflecting the harshness of the Puritan society in which the story unfolds.

1. **Somber and Morose**: The story deals with heavy themes such as sin, guilt, and punishment. These themes are mirrored in the tone, which often feels somber, melancholic, and introspective. This is evident right from the start, as Hawthorne describes the "ugly edifice" of the prison and the "rigid severity of the Puritanic code of law" (Hawthorne, 1850, Ch. 1).

2. **Critical and Ironic**: Hawthorne maintains a critical and sometimes ironic tone towards the Puritan society, as he examines its hypocrisies and harsh judgment. For instance, when the townspeople admire Hester's beautifully embroidered letter, it's an example of Hawthorne's ironic tone, as he points out the town's fascination with the very symbol of sin they imposed on Hester (Hawthorne, 1850, Ch. 5).

3. **Romantic and Descriptive**: Consistent with the Romantic movement of which Hawthorne was a part, the novel's tone sometimes shifts to become more contemplative, philosophical, and appreciative of the natural world. For example, Hawthorne's descriptions of the forest and brook where Hester and Dimmesdale meet are painted with a tone of beauty, mystery, and freedom (Hawthorne, 1850, Ch. 16 & Ch. 18).

4. **Dramatic and Tense**: During key moments of conflict, such as Dimmesdale's climactic public confession, the tone becomes more dramatic and intense, highlighting the emotional and moral struggles of the characters (Hawthorne, 1850, Ch. 23).

Hawthorne's tone throughout "The Scarlet Letter" effectively sets the mood of the novel, reinforces its themes, and shapes the reader's perception of the characters and their societal context.

WHAT ARE THE MOTIFS

Motifs are recurring structures, contrasts, or literary devices that help to develop and inform a text's major themes. In "The Scarlet Letter", Nathaniel Hawthorne uses several notable motifs to deepen his exploration of sin, guilt, and redemption. Here are a few:

1. **The Scarlet Letter**: The red "A" that Hester Prynne is forced to wear is a constant reminder of her sin and becomes a powerful motif in the novel. Initially standing for "Adulterer," the meanings of the scarlet letter change throughout the story, symbolizing "Able" among the townsfolk due to Hester's strength and resilience, or "Angel" during Governor Winthrop's death vigil (Hawthorne, 1850, Ch. 13 & Ch. 12).

2. **Night vs. Day**: Hawthorne often uses the contrast between night and day to explore the public and private selves of his characters. For instance, the scaffold scenes at the beginning and end of the novel happen at night, symbolic of the hidden guilt and sin, whereas the daytime represents the public exposure of sin and guilt (Hawthorne, 1850, Ch. 2, Ch. 23).

3. **The Meteor**: The meteor that lights up the sky as Dimmesdale stands on the scaffold in chapter 12 serves as a motif. The townsfolk believe it signifies "Angel" for Governor Winthrop's entry into heaven, but to Dimmesdale, it appears as an "A", reflecting his own guilt (Hawthorne, 1850, Ch. 12).

4. **The Wilderness vs. The Village**: The wilderness, where Hester and Dimmesdale can freely express their feelings, is a motif representing freedom and natural law. It is contrasted with the village, which represents civilization, social order, and confinement (Hawthorne, 1850, Ch. 16).

5. **The Rosebush**: The rosebush outside the prison, mentioned at the beginning of the novel, serves as a motif representing beauty and hope amidst a harsh and judgmental environment (Hawthorne, 1850, Ch. 1).

By utilizing these motifs throughout the novel, Hawthorne underscores the themes of sin, punishment, and ultimately the possibility of redemption.

What is the foreshadowing in the novel

Nathaniel Hawthorne uses foreshadowing in "The Scarlet Letter" to hint at future events and to build suspense. Here are some examples:

1. **Hester's Public Shame**: During Hester's initial public shaming, she sees her past husband (later known as Roger Chillingworth) in the crowd. He makes a gesture for her to keep his identity secret (Hawthorne, 1850, Ch. 3). This foreshadows Chillingworth's future role as an antagonist and the fact that he will be a cause of secret torment for both Hester and Dimmesdale.

2. **Pearl's Fascination with the Scarlet Letter**: From an early age, Pearl is intrigued by the scarlet letter on her mother's chest and occasionally acts out towards it (Hawthorne, 1850, Ch. 7). This foreshadows her role as the conscience of both Hester and Dimmesdale, reminding them of their sin.

3. **Dimmesdale's Health**: Dimmesdale's worsening health and his habit of holding his hand over his heart suggest a grave secret (Hawthorne, 1850, Ch. 10). These are foreshadowing his connection to Hester and the sin they share, which is revealed towards the end of the novel.

4. **The Meteor**: When Dimmesdale sees the meteor in the sky, he interprets it as a sign from God showing an "A" as in 'adulterer' (Hawthorne, 1850, Ch. 12). This foreshadows his ultimate public

confession of his sin of adultery.

5. **Chillingworth's Threat**: When Chillingworth tells Hester that the town fathers are considering letting her remove the scarlet letter and she should resist, he says that the scarlet letter will fall off on its own when it's time for her to take it off (Hawthorne, 1850, Ch. 14). This foreshadows the eventual removal of the letter after Dimmesdale's public confession.

By incorporating foreshadowing into his narrative, Hawthorne creates suspense and anticipation, which encourages readers to keep turning the pages to see how the hints and clues will unfold.

What is The Custom House

"The Custom House" is the introductory section of Nathaniel Hawthorne's novel "The Scarlet Letter." It serves as a kind of preface or prologue to the main narrative. Rather than jumping directly into the story of Hester Prynne and her scarlet letter, Hawthorne uses "The Custom House" to establish a narrative framework and provide context for the tale.

In "The Custom House," a semi-fictionalized version of Hawthorne himself is presented as the narrator, a surveyor working in the Custom House in Salem, Massachusetts. The Custom House is a place where taxes and duties were collected on imported goods, and the detailed description of the building and its workers serve as a commentary on bureaucracy and the political climate of the time.

The narrator discovers a piece of red cloth shaped like an 'A' along with some papers that detail the events of "The Scarlet Letter." He is fascinated by the scarlet letter and decides to write a fictional account based on the documents he finds, which becomes the novel "The Scarlet Letter."

"The Custom House" section serves several purposes. It provides a historical context and a sense of verisimilitude for the story, making it seem as though the events of "The Scarlet Letter" are based on real historical documents. It also allows Hawthorne to share his views on his contemporary society, his former job at the actual Custom House, and his thoughts on writing and creativity.

Hawthorne's decision to include this introduction has been a point of discussion among critics and scholars. Some argue that it distracts from the central narrative, while others maintain it provides important context and depth to the overall novel.

Summary of The Scarlet Letter

"The Scarlet Letter" by Nathaniel Hawthorne, published in 1850, is a work of historical fiction set in 17th-century Puritan Boston, Massachusetts.

Introduction and Hester's Punishment: The novel begins with an introduction by a narrator who happens upon a piece of fabric emblazoned with a gold and scarlet 'A' in an attic of the customs house. The story then proceeds to recount events that occurred around two centuries prior. Hester Prynne, a young woman, stands on a scaffold in the town square, holding an infant, Pearl. She is wearing a scarlet 'A' on her chest as a symbol of her adultery. Despite the public humiliation and the clergy's demands, Hester refuses to name the father of her child.

Roger Chillingworth's Intentions: Unbeknownst to the townspeople, Hester's husband, who had been presumed lost at sea, has arrived in town, having lived with Native Americans and taken the pseudonym Roger Chillingworth. After seeing Hester's shame, Chillingworth visits her in prison, where he convinces her to keep his identity a secret and vows to find the man with whom she committed adultery.

Hester's Life and Pearl's Childhood: After her release from prison, Hester lives on the outskirts of town, earning a living as a seamstress, and raises her daughter Pearl, who is described as being a passionate and unruly child. Hester is shunned by the townspeople and lives a lonely life.

Chillingworth and Dimmesdale's Relationship: Meanwhile, Reverend Arthur Dimmesdale, a respected young minister in the town, begins to suffer from an unknown ailment. Chillingworth, who is a physician, moves in with Dimmesdale under the guise of providing medical care. Over time, Chillingworth grows convinced that Dimmesdale is the unnamed father of Pearl. He begins to torment the guilt-ridden minister, subtly suggesting that he knows his secret.

Hester's Intervention and Plan: Seeing Dimmesdale's failing health and the psychological torture Chillingworth is inflicting, Hester decides to intervene. She confronts Chillingworth by the seaside, confesses that she has been concealing his identity, and begs for forgiveness. Chillingworth refuses to forgive her and insists that his revenge on the minister cannot be stopped.

Hester arranges a meeting with Dimmesdale in the forest. She reveals to him that Chillingworth is her husband. Stunned, Dimmesdale is filled with a mix of anger and relief. Hester then suggests that they escape to Europe where they can start anew. They plan to leave after Dimmesdale's Election Day sermon, a major event in the town. Pearl, who has been playing in the forest, is called over and finally meets her father.

Dimmesdale's Confession: On the day of the sermon, Dimmesdale delivers a passionate speech. After his sermon, he summons Hester and Pearl to join him on the scaffold. Here, before the townspeople, Dimmesdale confesses his sin and reveals a scarlet letter seared into his flesh. He dies on the scaffold after his confession.

Aftermath and Conclusion: Chillingworth, deprived of his victim, declines rapidly and dies within the year, leaving a sizeable inheritance to Pearl. Hester and Pearl leave Boston, and many years later, Hester returns alone. She lives out the remainder of her life in her old cottage and continues her charity work, eventually earning the townspeople's respect. She resumes wearing the scarlet letter as a symbol of her past sins and penance. When she dies, she is buried next to Dimmesdale, with the two sharing a single tombstone marked with the scarlet letter "A".

Pearl's Life: In the intervening years, Pearl, who has inherited wealth from Chillingworth, has married and is living in Europe. She maintains contact with Hester, often writing letters and occasionally sending gifts. It's suggested that Pearl has a family of her own, indicating a happier, more conventional life than the one she had during her childhood.

Hester's Legacy: Hester Prynne becomes something of a legend in the town. Her story is told and retold, with some townspeople suggesting that they see a spectral scarlet "A" in the sky, mirroring the letter she wore. Hester's experiences and resilience turn her into a figure of compassion, and she spends her final years offering comfort and advice to other women.

In this way, "The Scarlet Letter" concludes by tying up the fates of its central characters while leaving a lasting legacy of Hester's story that continues to echo through the town's history long after her death. The enduring power of the scarlet letter "A" and the narrative surrounding it encapsulate the novel's ongoing themes of sin, punishment, redemption, and the societal perception of morality.

Main characters

"The Scarlet Letter" by Nathaniel Hawthorne features several main characters:

1. Hester Prynne: The protagonist of the novel, Hester is a young woman sentenced to wear the scarlet letter 'A' on her chest as a punishment for committing adultery. She is the mother of Pearl, the product of her affair. Hester is a strong, compassionate woman who, despite public shaming and ostracism, retains her dignity and independence.

2. Pearl: Pearl is Hester's illegitimate daughter, who she raises alone. Pearl is described as a remarkably beautiful, vibrant, and willful child, with an almost unearthly quality. Throughout the novel, Pearl is seen as a living symbol of Hester's sin.

3. Arthur Dimmesdale: Dimmesdale is a revered young minister in the Puritan community of Boston who is later revealed to be Pearl's father. He struggles with his guilt for not admitting his sin and his love for Hester, which leads to both physical and mental health issues.

4. Roger Chillingworth: Chillingworth is Hester's husband who is presumed lost at sea when Hester is convicted. He arrives in Boston to witness Hester's public shaming and, keeping his identity a secret, vows to find the man who had an affair with his wife. He is later revealed as the novel's antagonist, who seeks revenge on Dimmesdale.

Describe Hester Prynne

Hester Prynne, the protagonist of Nathaniel Hawthorne's "The Scarlet Letter," is a complex character, representing strength, endurance, independence, and resilience against societal norms.

Description and Personality: Hester is described as a beautiful woman with dark and abundant hair, deep black eyes, and a figure marked by its "force and freedom" (Hawthorne, 1850, Ch. 2). She is dignified and composed, standing on the scaffold with a sense of resilience and defiance, refusing to let her punishment break her spirit.

Symbol of Adultery: As the novel begins, Hester is publicly shamed for committing adultery and is sentenced to wear a scarlet 'A' on her chest as a perpetual symbol of her sin. Despite her punishment, Hester refuses to name her child's father, displaying strength and loyalty (Hawthorne, 1850, Ch. 3).

Motherhood and Independence: Hester devotes herself to raising her daughter Pearl, who she sees as both a blessing and a reminder of her sin. She shows great independence and industriousness by providing for herself and Pearl through her skills as a seamstress (Hawthorne, 1850, Ch. 5).

Strength and Compassion: Despite societal ostracism, Hester carries herself with dignity and even uses her difficult experiences to develop compassion for others. She helps the poor and sick, demonstrating a strong moral character that contrasts with the sin for which she's been condemned (Hawthorne, 1850, Ch. 13).

Conflict and Resolution: Hester experiences internal conflict over her feelings for Dimmesdale and her anger toward Chillingworth. Eventually, she helps Dimmesdale to confess his part in their shared sin, demonstrating her belief in truth and redemption (Hawthorne, 1850, Ch. 17-20).

Endurance and Legacy: By the end of the novel, Hester returns to Boston after some years spent abroad, choosing to continue wearing the scarlet letter. She spends her remaining years providing comfort and counsel to other women, thus changing the meaning of the scarlet letter from a symbol of shame to one of resilience and empathy (Hawthorne, 1850, Conclusion).

Describe Hester as a tragic character

Hester Prynne from Nathaniel Hawthorne's "The Scarlet Letter" can be seen as a tragic character due to the enduring consequences she faces for her forbidden love, her societal isolation, and the torment she experiences due to the secrecy surrounding her situation.

Love and Punishment: The root of Hester's tragedy lies in her affair with Arthur Dimmesdale. Their love, deemed illicit by the Puritan society in which they live, leads to Hester's public humiliation and continual punishment. She is forced to wear the scarlet letter 'A' on her chest, a constant reminder of her "sin" of adultery (Hawthorne, 1850, Ch. 2).

Societal Isolation: Hester's punishment doesn't end with the scarlet letter. She's ostracized from society, living on the outskirts of town, and struggles to raise her daughter Pearl in isolation. This constant exclusion represents a daily tragic struggle against societal norms (Hawthorne, 1850, Ch. 5).

Unrequited Love and Secrecy: Hester's love for Dimmesdale remains unrequited in a conventional sense due to his inability to confess his part in the adultery due to fear and guilt. The fact that she must keep this love and Dimmesdale's identity as Pearl's father a secret exacerbates her tragic circumstances (Hawthorne, 1850, Ch. 4).

Roger Chillingworth: Hester's husband, assuming the name Roger Chillingworth, adds another layer to her tragic experience. He vows to find the man who dishonored him and becomes a constant tormentor of Dimmesdale, Hester's unacknowledged love. Despite recognizing Chillingworth's revengeful intent, Hester is bound by her promise to keep his identity secret, adding to her emotional torment (Hawthorne, 1850, Ch. 4).

Endurance and Redemption: However, Hester's tragedy is not one of downfall. Unlike typical tragic heroes who meet a disastrous end, Hester endures her suffering and strives to find redemption and acceptance. After Dimmesdale's death, she leaves Boston, but eventually returns, willingly wearing her scarlet letter. She transforms her symbol of shame into a symbol of individuality and resilience, providing help and counsel to other women (Hawthorne, 1850, Conclusion).

While Hester experiences a series of tragic circumstances, her endurance and resilience offer a more optimistic perspective on her character, marking her as a tragic but ultimately triumphant heroine.

Describe Arthur Dimmesdale

Arthur Dimmesdale, one of the main characters in Nathaniel Hawthorne's "The Scarlet Letter," is a respected Puritan minister who conceals his role in Hester Prynne's adultery, leading to dramatic internal conflict and deteriorating health.

Role and Reputation: Dimmesdale is a young, eloquent, and well-respected minister in Boston, highly esteemed by his congregation for his apparent virtue and piety (Hawthorne, 1850, Ch. 3).

Secret Sin and Guilt: While Dimmesdale is widely revered, he conceals a secret sin. He is Pearl's father, which means he committed adultery with Hester. Yet, unlike Hester, who publicly wears the mark of their sin, he hides his guilt. This guilt and hypocrisy eat away at him, leading to both physical and psychological suffering (Hawthorne, 1850, Ch. 11).

Dimmesdale's Health and Chillingworth: Dimmesdale's guilt manifests as declining health. He frequently clutches his chest, a physical manifestation of his internal torment. Chillingworth, who is actually Hester's husband seeking revenge, becomes Dimmesdale's doctor and intensifies his guilt and torment (Hawthorne, 1850, Ch. 10).

Pearl and Hester's Influence: Dimmesdale shares a connection with Hester and Pearl. Pearl, in her intuitive, perceptive manner, questions Dimmesdale about his habit of placing his hand over his heart, hinting at their shared secret (Hawthorne, 1850, Ch. 15). Hester, despite his role in her public shame, still loves him and convinces him to confess his sin (Hawthorne, 1850, Ch. 17).

Confession and Death: Towards the novel's climax, Dimmesdale finally confesses his sin before his congregation, revealing a scarlet letter on his chest. This act of confession and public humiliation is also his final act, as he dies soon afterward, finally finding release from his guilt (Hawthorne, 1850, Ch. 23).

Symbolism: Dimmesdale's character represents the destructive power of hidden guilt and the struggle between one's public persona and private sins. His confession and subsequent death show the tragic consequences of his choices.

Describe Roger Chillingworth

Roger Chillingworth, one of the central characters in Nathaniel Hawthorne's "The Scarlet Letter," is Hester Prynne's husband who is transformed by his quest for revenge. Initially a scholar, his identity and personality dramatically change throughout the novel.

Initial Appearance and Background: Chillingworth is initially introduced as a stranger witnessing Hester's public humiliation. He is an older, misshapen man, stooped and scholarly. Before the novel's timeline, he sent Hester to Boston while he finished some business in Europe. He was believed to be lost at sea until he appears in Boston (Hawthorne, 1850, Ch. 3).

Identity and Relationship with Hester: Chillingworth is revealed to be Hester's husband, though he asks her to keep his identity secret. They share a brief conversation where he admits they wronged each other: him for marrying a young, vibrant woman despite his age and deformity, and her for marrying him without love and then committing adultery (Hawthorne, 1850, Ch. 4).

Revenge and Transformation: When he finds out about Hester's adultery, Chillingworth devotes himself to discovering and tormenting her lover. This mission transforms him, and he evolves from a wronged husband into a villain bent on revenge. Hawthorne suggests that this transformation is so profound that even his physical appearance changes, becoming more evil and sinister (Hawthorne, 1850, Ch. 9-10).

Relationship with Dimmesdale: Chillingworth manages to become close to the ailing Reverend Dimmesdale under the guise of a physician. He realizes that Dimmesdale is Pearl's father and torments him psychologically, driving the minister towards physical and mental deterioration (Hawthorne, 1850, Ch. 10 & Ch. 14).

Dimmesdale's Confession and Death: Chillingworth's plans are thwarted when Dimmesdale confesses his sin to the public and dies, thus escaping his tormentor's clutches. Chillingworth dies within the year, his life seemingly devoid of purpose without his revenge (Hawthorne, 1850, Ch. 23 & Ch. 24).

Legacy and Redemption: In a final attempt at redemption, Chillingworth leaves his property to Pearl, providing her with financial security. This final act suggests a glimmer of humanity within him (Hawthorne, 1850, Ch. 24).

Symbolism: Chillingworth can be seen as a symbol of evil and revenge. His transformation into a figure driven by vengeance demonstrates the destructive power of unrelenting anger and resentment.

Describe Pearl

Pearl, the daughter of Hester Prynne and Arthur Dimmesdale in Nathaniel Hawthorne's "The Scarlet Letter," is a crucial character whose existence drives the plot and symbolizes various themes throughout the novel.

Appearance and Initial Description: Pearl is first described as an extremely beautiful child with an "airy sprite" like quality. She possesses her mother's beauty and fiery, passionate hair, shining with "a deep, rich luster, that perfectly assimilated with the hue of the dress" (Hawthorne, 1850, Ch. 6).

Symbol of Hester's Sin: Pearl serves as a living reminder of Hester's 'sin' of adultery. Hawthorne directly refers to Pearl as "the scarlet letter endowed with life" (Hawthorne, 1850, Ch. 7). Hester herself acknowledges this when she says, "She is my happiness!—she is my torture, nonetheless! Pearl keeps me here in life!" (Hawthorne, 1850, Ch. 8).

Temperament and Mischief: Pearl is often described as mischievous and 'wild.' She can be seen as a mirror of the wild, untamed, and natural passions that led to her conception. She doesn't conform to the Puritan society's strict and repressive norms, and her behavior often reflects her nonconformist spirit (Hawthorne, 1850, Ch. 6).

Pearl and the Scarlet Letter: Pearl shows an odd fascination with the scarlet 'A' on her mother's bosom from a very early age. This represents her innate understanding of her mother's and her own marginalized place in the Puritan society (Hawthorne, 1850, Ch. 7).

Understanding Her Parents' Secret: Despite her young age, Pearl seems to sense the unspoken connection between Dimmesdale and her mother. She repeatedly asks about the "Black Man" (symbolizing the devil and sin in Puritan folklore) and Dimmesdale's habit of placing his hand over his heart (Hawthorne, 1850, Ch. 15 & Ch. 19). This demonstrates her uncanny perception of the unspoken guilt and secret her parents share.

Pearl's Redemption: In thc forest scene, when Dimmesdale finally publicly acknowledges Pearl as his daughter, she is allowed to express her affection towards him, marking a moment of emotional release. It's after this point that she is seen to become a "normal" child, no longer serving just as a symbol of her mother's sin (Hawthorne, 1850, Ch. 19).

Pearl's Future: At the end of the novel, it is implied that Pearl lives a fulfilled life in Europe, marries, and possibly has a family of her own. She also inherits wealth from Chillingworth. However, despite her distance, Pearl continues to maintain contact with Hester, showing their enduring mother-daughter bond (Hawthorne, 1850, Conclusion).

Describe Hester's relationship with Arthur and Roger

In Nathaniel Hawthorne's "The Scarlet Letter," Hester Prynne's relationships with Arthur Dimmesdale and Roger Chillingworth are central to the novel's plot and themes.

Hester's Relationship with Arthur Dimmesdale:

Hester and Arthur share a forbidden love, as they conceived a child, Pearl, while Hester was still married to Chillingworth, and Arthur was a minister of their church. They keep their relationship a secret due to the grave repercussions they would face from their Puritan society. This secret significantly impacts their lives:

- **Love and Sin**: Hester and Arthur's relationship is portrayed as genuine love, but it is also categorized as sin within their society. This tension between personal feelings and societal norms creates a moral quandary that is central to the novel (Hawthorne, 1850, Ch. 4).

- **Guilt and Suffering**: Both Hester and Arthur suffer due to their relationship. Hester endures public humiliation and social ostracization, while Arthur suffers from guilt, which results in physical and mental deterioration (Hawthorne, 1850, Ch. 2, Ch. 11).

- **Connection through Pearl**: Their daughter, Pearl, represents their love but also serves as a constant reminder of their sin. Pearl's existence perpetuates their connection, despite their efforts to lead separate lives (Hawthorne, 1850, Ch. 6).

Hester's Relationship with Roger Chillingworth:

Hester and Chillingworth were married in Europe, but it was not a marriage of love. Chillingworth sent Hester ahead to America while he settled some affairs, but he arrived later than expected, by which time Hester had already begun her affair with Arthur.

- **Marriage and Discontent**: Their marriage is portrayed as one of convenience rather than love. Hester admits to Chillingworth that she never loved him, highlighting the lack of affection in their relationship (Hawthorne, 1850, Ch. 4).

- **Betrayal and Revenge**: Upon learning that Hester has had an affair, Chillingworth seeks revenge, not directly on Hester, but on her unknown lover. His quest for vengeance transforms him into a malevolent figure, embodying the destructive power of revenge (Hawthorne, 1850, Ch. 4, Ch. 14).

- **Power and Control**: Chillingworth manipulates Hester by insisting she must not reveal his true identity. This gives him control over her, adding an element of power imbalance in their relationship (Hawthorne, 1850, Ch. 4).

Overall, Hester's relationships with Arthur and Roger reflect the novel's themes of sin, guilt, revenge, and the struggle between personal desires and societal expectations.

MINOR CHARACTERS

"The Scarlet Letter" by Nathaniel Hawthorne contains several minor characters who, while not as central as Hester Prynne, Arthur Dimmesdale, Pearl, and Roger Chillingworth, significantly contribute to the story and its themes.

The Townspeople and the Women of Boston: The townspeople serve as a collective character that represents the Puritan society of 17th-century Boston. They initially react with scorn and judgment towards Hester, enforcing her public shaming and ostracization. Their attitudes provide a stark contrast to Hester's individualism and highlight the oppressive moral codes of the time (Hawthorne, 1850, Ch. 2).

Governor Bellingham: As the governor of the Massachusetts Bay Colony, Bellingham represents the government and its legal and religious authority. He is part of the group of men who judge Hester during her public shaming and later questions Hester's ability to raise Pearl due to the child's unconventional behavior. His actions contribute to Hester's struggle and isolation (Hawthorne, 1850, Ch. 2 & Ch. 8).

Mistress Hibbins: Mistress Hibbins, who is depicted as a witch consorting with the "Black Man" (the devil), symbolizes the subversive elements within Puritan society. Her invitation to Hester to join her in the forest symbolizes the temptation for Hester to abandon societal norms completely. Mistress Hibbins also serves as a counterpoint to Hester, showing the extent to which the community marginalizes those who do not conform to its strict moral code (Hawthorne, 1850, Ch. 8 & Ch. 15).

Rev. John Wilson: Reverend Wilson is the elder clergyman of Boston and another figure of religious authority. He is the one who urges Dimmesdale to demand from Hester the name of her child's father during her time on the scaffold. His character represents the rigid religious authority of Puritan society and its judgment (Hawthorne, 1850, Ch. 3).

The Ship's Captain: The ship's captain tells Hester that Chillingworth also booked passage on the ship to Europe where Hester and Pearl plan to start anew, heightening the sense of dread and inevitability towards the novel's climax (Hawthorne, 1850, Ch. 21 & Ch. 22).

These characters, though minor in terms of their presence in the narrative, play significant roles in illustrating the societal context, moral codes, and central conflicts surrounding the main characters.

Describe Governor Bellingham

Governor Richard Bellingham is a minor character in Nathaniel Hawthorne's "The Scarlet Letter." He represents the Puritan civil authority in the Massachusetts Bay Colony.

Governor Bellingham is described as elderly and a little pompous. He is a very formal and proper character, often dressed in ornate and grand clothing, in contrast with the stark simplicity typically associated with the Puritans. Hawthorne uses him to depict the contradiction and hypocrisy within the Puritan society — the difference between their espoused values of simplicity and humility, and the grandeur with which they adorn themselves.

He is one of the men who pass judgment on Hester Prynne at the beginning of the story, highlighting the strict moral code of Puritan society (Hawthorne, 1850, Ch. 2). Later in the novel, he also questions Hester's fitness as a mother and threatens to separate her from her daughter, Pearl. His sternness and judgment further exemplify the oppressive societal norms that Hester battles against (Hawthorne, 1850, Ch. 8).

Despite his rigid judgment of others, Bellingham is shown to be quite fond of his sister, Mistress Hibbins, who is rumored to be a witch, indicating a contradiction in his character and further highlighting the underlying hypocrisy within Puritan society (Hawthorne, 1850, Ch. 8).

Describe Mistress Hibbins

Mistress Hibbins is a minor character in Nathaniel Hawthorne's "The Scarlet Letter." She is presented as a witch who is frequently interacting with the Devil and is also the sister of Governor Bellingham, a symbol of Puritan authority.

Hawthorne uses Mistress Hibbins to explore the theme of hidden wickedness in the seemingly virtuous Puritan society. Her character's presence suggests a dual nature within the Puritan community, where behind the facade of righteousness, darker elements lurk. Despite her brother's standing, her nefarious activities go unpunished, highlighting the double standards and hypocrisy within society.

She appears at key moments in the novel, such as after the Governor's party, where she invites Hester to join her in the forest for a meeting with the Devil (Hawthorne, 1850, Ch. 8). This encounter underscores the thematic connection between Hester's scarlet letter (sin) and the idea of witchcraft.

Mistress Hibbins also appears at the end of the novel, after Dimmesdale's death, suggesting that she knows of his secret sin (Hawthorne, 1850, Ch. 24). Her insinuations add an eerie and mysterious layer to the novel, contributing to the overall sense of guilt, hidden sin, and duplicity.

Hawthorne based the character of Mistress Hibbins on a historical figure, Ann Hibbins, who was executed for witchcraft in Boston in 1656, a few years after the period in which the novel is set.

Who is the hero of the novel

The hero of a novel is often a subjective designation that depends on how the reader interprets the story. In Nathaniel Hawthorne's "The Scarlet Letter," different characters display heroic traits and play central roles in the narrative, but the term 'hero' can be most fittingly applied to Hester Prynne, depending on one's interpretation of the novel.

Hester Prynne: As the protagonist of "The Scarlet Letter," Hester Prynne displays considerable resilience and moral strength. Despite public shame and ostracism due to her adulterous affair, Hester maintains her dignity and refuses to name her child's father, which shows her loyalty. Her independent spirit and the courage to live on her terms, in spite of societal norms, demonstrate her heroism.

Moreover, Hester shows her strength and selflessness through her actions. She uses her talents as a seamstress not only to support herself and her daughter Pearl but also to help the poor. As time goes by, many townspeople begin to associate her scarlet letter 'A' not with 'adultery,' but with 'able.'

Despite her sin, Hester is the character who evolves the most in the novel, turning her punishment into a powerful symbol of identity, and thus could be seen as the story's hero.

However, this designation doesn't mean that other characters, such as Arthur Dimmesdale or even Pearl, don't have moments of bravery or importance. Instead, it emphasizes Hester's central role in the narrative and her embodiment of the book's main themes.

What literary style was used

Nathaniel Hawthorne employs a rich and complex style in his novel "The Scarlet Letter," drawing from several stylistic approaches. Here are specific examples from the novel to illustrate:

1. **Symbolism**: Hawthorne makes extensive use of symbolism. The scarlet letter "A" is the most obvious symbol, initially representing "adulteress" but evolving in meaning throughout the story, even taking on the meaning "able" among the town's people (Hawthorne, 1850, Ch. 13).

2. **Allegory**: Hawthorne uses allegory throughout, with characters and plot developments standing in for broader moral or philosophical concepts. For instance, Pearl is not only Hester's daughter but also a living embodiment of her sin and a symbol of consequence and truth (Hawthorne, 1850, Ch. 6).

3. **Psychological Realism**: Hawthorne delves into the inner lives and struggles of his characters, particularly Hester Prynne and Arthur Dimmesdale. Their guilt, suffering, and inner conflict are vividly portrayed, such as when Dimmesdale tortures himself in his closet for his unconfessed sin (Hawthorne, 1850, Ch. 11).

4. **Detailed Descriptions and Dense Prose**: Hawthorne's descriptive prose style is evident throughout the novel, as he describes settings, characters, and emotions with great detail and intricate

language. For example, the opening chapter's detailed description of the prison door and its surroundings establishes a somber mood and setting (Hawthorne, 1850, Ch. 1).

5. **Historical and Cultural References**: Hawthorne immerses the reader in the world of Puritan New England through specific historical and cultural references, as seen in the depiction of the community's strict moral code and how it governs the lives of its inhabitants (Hawthorne, 1850, throughout).

6. **Frame Narrative**: Hawthorne employs a frame narrative in "The Scarlet Letter." The novel begins with an introductory essay called "The Custom-House," in which Hawthorne, in the voice of a semi-fictionalized version of himself, discovers the scarlet letter and the story behind it. This "story within a story" approach adds another layer to the novel's narrative complexity. (Hawthorne, 1850, "The Custom House").

Hawthorne's style in "The Scarlet Letter" serves to heighten the novel's exploration of themes such as sin, guilt, hypocrisy, and redemption, while also providing a thorough examination of the human condition.

What genre is the novel

Nathaniel Hawthorne's "The Scarlet Letter" is generally classified within several overlapping genres:

1. **Historical Fiction**: "The Scarlet Letter" is set in the mid-17th century Puritan settlement of Boston, Massachusetts, a time and place that Hawthorne meticulously recreates using historical details (Hawthorne, 1850, Author's Preface).

2. **Romanticism**: The novel is often categorized as part of the Romantic literary movement, with its emphasis on individual experience, emotion, and the natural world. Hawthorne, like other Romantic writers, delves into the inner workings of the characters' minds, focuses on their moral and psychological struggles, and uses symbolism and nature as integral aspects of the narrative (Hawthorne, 1850, throughout).

3. **Gothic Fiction**: "The Scarlet Letter" also has elements of Gothic fiction, a sub-genre of Romanticism, including a dark and gloomy atmosphere, a focus on the supernatural (e.g., the witchcraft subplot), and a deep dive into the darker aspects of human nature (Hawthorne, 1850, Ch. 8, Ch. 12).

4. **Psychological Novel**: The novel could also be seen as a psychological novel due to its emphasis on the internal states and motivations of the characters. Hawthorne delves into the mental anguish

and guilt experienced by Hester Prynne and Arthur Dimmesdale, and the revenge obsession of Roger Chillingworth (Hawthorne, 1850, throughout).

What symbolism was used

Nathaniel Hawthorne employs various symbols throughout "The Scarlet Letter" to underscore the novel's themes of sin, guilt, punishment, and redemption. Here are some of the primary symbols:

1. **The Scarlet Letter**: The most obvious symbol in the novel is the scarlet letter "A" itself. Initially, it stands for "Adulteress," marking Hester for her sin. However, over time, the meaning of the letter shifts. It becomes a symbol of Hester's resilience and strength, her ability to overcome the stigma of her sin and reshape her identity. Some townspeople even suggest that it stands for "Able" (Hawthorne, 1850, Ch. 13).

2. **Pearl**: Hester's daughter Pearl is a living symbol of her sin - the product of the adulterous act. She's described as a kind of elfish sprite, often associated with natural elements and the supernatural, embodying the untamed and unrepentant nature of Hester's transgression. Pearl is also a symbol of truth in the novel, as she consistently refuses to let Dimmesdale hide his relationship to her and her mother (Hawthorne, 1850, Ch. 19).

3. **The Scaffold**: The scaffold is a symbol of public shame and punishment, as it's the place where Hester is first presented with her scarlet letter and where she stands with Dimmesdale and Pearl during Dimmesdale's public confession. Yet, it also becomes a site of redemption and reconciliation (Hawthorne, 1850, Ch. 12 &

Ch. 23).

4. **The Forest and the Town**: The town and the forest represent two opposing moral universes. The town, with its strict laws and severe moral code, contrasts with the wild, unruly, and free nature of the forest. The forest is where Hester and Dimmesdale can meet and express their love freely, and it's also associated with the perceived "evil" of the native inhabitants and Mistress Hibbins's witchcraft (Hawthorne, 1850, Ch. 16 & Ch. 18).

5. **The Meteor**: The meteor that lights up the sky when Dimmesdale stands on the scaffold, perceived by the minister to be an "A" for "adultery," is a symbol of his guilt. However, the townspeople interpret it as an "A" for "Angel" marking the death of Governor Winthrop, further highlighting the novel's theme of differing perspectives (Hawthorne, 1850, Ch. 12).

Describe the novel's conflicts

In Nathaniel Hawthorne's "The Scarlet Letter," there are several conflicts, both external and internal, that drive the narrative. The novel explores these conflicts through the struggles of its main characters: Hester Prynne, Arthur Dimmesdale, and Roger Chillingworth.

1. **Hester's Conflict with Society (External)**: Hester's main conflict stems from her act of adultery, which is a grave sin in her Puritan society. She's publicly shamed and required to wear the scarlet letter "A" on her dress as a symbol of her sin (Hawthorne, 1850, Ch. 2 & Ch. 3). This conflict shapes Hester's experiences and influences her relationships with others, forcing her to grapple with societal norms and expectations.

2. **Hester's Inner Conflict (Internal)**: Hester experiences internal conflict regarding her feelings for Dimmesdale and Chillingworth. She wrestles with her love for Dimmesdale, despite the societal norms they have violated, and her feelings of resentment towards her husband, Chillingworth, for his desire for revenge (Hawthorne, 1850, Ch. 4, Ch. 17).

3. **Dimmesdale's Inner Conflict (Internal)**: Reverend Dimmesdale, Pearl's father and Hester's lover, experiences intense guilt for his sin and for letting Hester bear the brunt of their shared transgression. His guilt manifests in self-punishment and illness, revealing the torment of his moral and spiritual conflict

(Hawthorne, 1850, Ch. 11 & Ch. 12).

4. **Chillingworth's Conflict with Dimmesdale (External)**: Chillingworth, Hester's husband, devotes himself to seeking revenge against the man who fathered Hester's child. He learns that Dimmesdale is the man he's been seeking and torments him, leading to an external conflict that drives much of the narrative's suspense and tragedy (Hawthorne, 1850, Ch. 10 & Ch. 14).

5. **Society's Conflict with Itself (External)**: The rigid moral codes of the Puritan society are also portrayed as being in conflict with the reality of human nature. The strict laws and unyielding religious values lead to intense societal pressure and hypocrisy, contributing to the central characters' conflicts and sufferings (Hawthorne, 1850, throughout).

The various conflicts in "The Scarlet Letter" serve to highlight the novel's central themes of sin, guilt, and the conflict between personal feelings and societal norms.

What is the climax

The climax of "The Scarlet Letter" by Nathaniel Hawthorne is typically identified as the scene in Chapter 23, "The Revelation of the Scarlet Letter." This is the moment when Reverend Arthur Dimmesdale, during the Election Day sermon, confesses his sin to the Puritan community.

Here's how this scene unfolds:

Dimmesdale has just finished delivering what the crowd believes to be his most powerful sermon yet. However, instead of descending from the pulpit, Dimmesdale calls Hester and Pearl to join him on the scaffold. In this public square, he confesses that he is Pearl's father, the one who shared in Hester's sin of adultery (Hawthorne, 1850, Ch. 23).

This is the moment of greatest emotional intensity in the novel. It is the climax because it is the turning point that resolves the central conflict. Dimmesdale's confession releases him from his internal torment, but it also comes with a high price—his life. Immediately after confessing his sin, Dimmesdale dies on the scaffold, leaving Hester and Pearl in the crowd (Hawthorne, 1850, Ch. 23).

This scene is also the climax because it provides a stark contrast to the initial scaffold scene. While Hester had stood alone in her public shaming at the beginning of the novel, in this climactic scene, she shares the platform with Dimmesdale and Pearl, suggesting a moment of collective redemption and defiance against the oppressive Puritan society.

What is the moral of the story

Nathaniel Hawthorne's "The Scarlet Letter" is a complex novel that explores many themes, allowing for multiple interpretations of its moral message. Here are a few key morals that readers may glean from the book:

1. **The Destructiveness of Secret Sin**: The novel illustrates the psychological toll and physical deterioration that can result from hidden guilt and sin. Reverend Dimmesdale's torment and eventual death demonstrate the damaging effects of his unconfessed sin. This moral suggests that confession and atonement are necessary steps to find peace and redemption.

2. **The Hypocrisy of Society**: The story reveals the hypocrisy and rigid moralism of Puritan society. The same community members who condemn Hester for her sin are themselves flawed individuals. This highlights the moral that societal norms can often be inflexible and unfairly punitive, and that society is often too quick to judge others.

3. **The Strength of Individualism**: Hester Prynne is a symbol of resilience and strength. Despite her ostracization, she builds a life for herself and her daughter Pearl, challenging societal norms and expectations. This suggests a moral about the power of personal strength and the importance of defining one's own identity, even in the face of societal condemnation.

4. **The Consequences of Revenge**: Roger Chillingworth's pursuit of revenge transforms him into a person solely driven by spite and malice, ultimately leading to a miserable existence. This theme presents a moral warning against the destructive path of revenge.

5. **The Potential for Transformation**: The scarlet letter, initially a symbol of shame, over time, becomes associated with "able", suggesting Hester's strong character and ability. This shows the potential for personal transformation and the capacity to redefine one's identity despite societal labels or past mistakes.

The exact moral of "The Scarlet Letter" can vary depending on the reader's interpretation, as Hawthorne leaves much of the novel's deeper meaning open-ended, allowing for these and other morals to be drawn from his work.

Memorable Quotes

Quote: "It is remarkable, that persons who speculate the most boldly often conform with the most perfect quietude to the external regulations of society."

1. **Reference**: Preface.
2. **Importance**: Highlights the theme of hypocrisy within Puritan society, suggesting that the most intellectually free individuals may still adhere strictly to societal norms, underlining the discrepancy between public appearance and private identity.

Quote: "The scarlet letter was her passport into regions where other women dared not tread."

1. **Reference**: Ch. 18.
2. **Importance**: Signifies Hester's transformation and the duality of the scarlet letter as both a mark of shame and a symbol of resilience and unique strength, allowing her access to freedoms and insights unavailable to others.

Quote: "She had not known the weight until she felt the freedom."

1. **Reference**: Ch. 18.
2. **Importance**: Emphasizes the oppressive nature of societal expectations and the enlightening experience of freedom from these burdens, underscoring the themes of oppression and liberation.

Quote: "We dream in our waking moments, and walk in our sleep."

1. **Reference**: Ch. 12.

2. **Importance**: Reflects the blurred boundaries between reality and illusion, capturing the characters' internal struggles and the dissonance between their public facades and private selves.

Quote: "No man for any considerable period can wear one face to himself, and another to the multitude, without finally getting bewildered as to which may be the true."

1. **Reference**: Ch. 20.

2. **Importance**: Addresses the theme of identity and the psychological damage caused by living a lie, particularly in the context of Dimmesdale's internal conflict and societal critique of hypocrisy.

Quote: "The world's law was no law for her mind."

1. **Reference**: Ch. 5.

2. **Importance**: This statement underscores Hester Prynne's inner strength and moral autonomy, highlighting her rejection of societal judgment and norms in favor of her own ethical compass, thereby challenging the rigid Puritanical laws and suggesting a broader critique of societal constraints on individual freedom.

Quote: "It is a curious subject of observation and inquiry, whether hatred and love be not the same thing at bottom."

1. **Reference**: Ch. 9.

2. **Importance**: Raises philosophical questions about the nature of human emotions and relationships, especially in the context of Roger Chillingworth's complex feelings towards Hester and Dimmesdale. It reflects on the thin line between love and hate,

suggesting a deeper exploration of human motivations and the capacity for both redemption and destruction.

Quote: "All the world had frowned on her – for seven long years had it frowned upon this lonely woman – and still she bore it all, nor ever once turned away her firm, sad eyes."

1. **Reference**: 13.

2. **Importance**: This highlights Hester's resilience and unwavering spirit in the face of continuous societal condemnation. It showcases her strength and dignity, emphasizing the novel's themes of punishment, isolation, and the endurance of the human spirit.

Quote: "There is no good on earth; and sin is but a name. Come, sinner, for thee, too, have I sought all these years!"

1. **Reference**: Ch. 20.

2. **Importance**: Spoken by the character of Mistress Hibbins, this quote delves into the novel's exploration of the relative nature of sin and virtue, challenging Puritanical black-and-white morality. It invites readers to question the societal definitions of good and evil, suggesting a more complex understanding of human actions and morality.

Through these quotes, Hawthorne intricately weaves a narrative rich with identity, freedom, sin, and redemption themes. Each quote stands out for its direct insight into the characters' struggles and societal commentary and contributes to the overarching moral and ethical exploration that defines "The Scarlet Letter."

About the Author

Steven Smith has written two dozen study guides as of this writing. The author is an educator and lifelong student, having studied at universities in Canada and the UK. His passion for teaching literature led him to create the Classic Books Explained series. His favourite book genres are historical fiction and nonfiction, as well as timeless classics like the ones covered in this series. Steven's inspiration to become an educator comes from his wife, who is a university professor. They have two children, a Jack Russell Terrier, and two rescued cats.

SD - #0028 - 070726 - C0 - 229/152/4 - PB - 9781964189758 - Matt Lamination